Wine Making for the Total Novice

By Kyle Richards

Table of Contents

Introduction 1
Some Wine History 3
Interesting Bits of Facts 7
The Benefits Of Wine 11
The Process of Winemaking 13
Different Kinds of Wine 17
Wine Tasting 25
The Benefits of Making Your Own Wine 27
Common Misconceptions 29
What Kind of Grapes Do I Use? 33
What Kind of Equipment Do I Need? 35
What About Sanitization? 39
Time to Make the Wine 43
Common Mistakes 47
Conclusion 49

Introduction

Have you been curious about how to make wine at home? What kinds of grapes are used? What type of equipment is needed? Is it expensive to get that equipment? Is it a difficult process to do at home successfully?

This book is for those who have never made wine before, a total novice to the process. It answers these questions for you in clear, concise steps and walks you through how to make your own first batch of wine.

You will also learn interesting facts and history about wine to help equip you with even more knowledge of this new endeavor.

How exciting this new adventure could be! Imagine serving your guests some great tasting wine that you made yourself, great food to accompany it, and loved ones to enjoy it with you.

Relish the journey, read on.

Some Wine History

"Either give me more wine or leave me alone." — Rumi

Throughout history, wine has been man's constant companion. In defeat and in victory, in disaster and in glory, wine has served both as a comfort and a trophy. History is seldom told without the mention of wine. Alliances are often celebrated through parties with wine in abundance.

The first indication of it is in circa 7000, in China. Evidence of the use of grapes with fermented rice and honey were unearthed. Then more evidence was found scattered across the Near East and in Europe. The existence of grape skins, stems, seeds, and stalks in an archeological location does not prove the making of wine, hence making it difficult to come up with a conclusive truth as to where production originated.

This fermented juice is important to the countries in the Middle East and essential to civilizations founded by the Greeks and the Romans. Great plantations have risen, and different methods of production and techniques when it comes to flavor, have been a constant challenge and have evolved to become an art in their own right.

Around 6000 BC, wine came to Europe when the Greek civilization spread around the globe. Wine has its place in the center of Greek culture. It was their doctors who first prescribed it to patients.

Viniculture, on the other hand, was improved and evolved into an industry, not to mention a science, when the Romans began to classify grapes in different categories based on factors such as variety, color, and soil preferences. Pruning, irrigation, and fertilization were given more attention, which resulted in harvests being maximized and increased.

The first century marks the export era for wines. Rome, being a strong empire, exported thousands of barrels in different ports around the globe. It is even believed that The Roman era was the first to use glass bottles as containers. France gained dominance in the market, and imports were forbidden. Many wine historians thank the monastic communities for the preservation and cultivation of the various techniques that are still applied today. Wine is also an important part in most of their religious rites.

The 14th and the 15th centuries were an open door for France's competitors in the export market since the trade between England and France was cut off due to political reasons.

Further quests for territory and dominion brought wine to South America and South Africa in the 1500s and 1600s. During this period, efforts to grow vineyards along the Atlantic and Gulf Coasts of North America were made with no success.

The earliest civilizations were founded in places where water was abundant. Economic growth and military power are dependent on natural resources; thus communities with ample supplies of basic necessities were able to build strong empires and wealthy nations.

It can be argued, however, that even though most civilizations are rooted in fountains and streams of water, wine was the necessary tool by which these civilizations were built.

Alliances were formed with wines and pacts. Royalty was measured in the abundance of a banquet and the quality of the wine. If you want to impress a ruler, a good wine is a good place to start.

Wine has been a hard worker's treat after a day of hard labor. An indispensable item in an important family dinner, wine is one of the highlights of a celebration, whether simple or grand.

The growth of cultures can be attributed to wine, too. From a friendly conversation of everyday things to matters of passion for a cause, wine has served as the springboard of beliefs and traditions. It is enjoyed by the many philosophers and even the world's modern thinkers, endorsed by artists and creative minds.

Plagues and political obstacles were not able to bring the wine industry down. With many risks, whether for the love of wine or love of money, taken by those who are known today as wine heroes, winemaking continues to grow both as a business opportunity and a pleasurable hobby.

There has never been a time when more people have consumed wine in great quantities and diversity. Production and consumption has greatly increased from the time of the European expansion up to today's countless acres of vineyards with specialty wines.

Technology has made it easier for wine producers to try different methods, and yet the same has made the field extremely competitive, as the number of wine enthusiasts has increased and the consumers' tastes have become more sophisticated and more diverse.

Interesting Bits of Facts

Being one of the world's oldest beverages that still exists today and having become a symbol of status and affluence, wine has a lot of stories up its sleeves. Here is a rundown of some of the most interesting facts gathered about this drink called wine.

The Chinese, as it turns out, are not only fond of tea, but also of wine. They are the biggest wine consumers. It was, however, in Germany that the oldest bottle of wine was unearthed. The bottle, which was dug up in 1867, was dated around 325 A.D.

The method of wine making was preserved by monks during the time when the whole industry of alcoholic beverages was at risk. Another fact of interest about wines is their names. For a beginner, the names might be a bit hard to pronounce in many cases. Names, as it turns out, indicate the location of the production and the variety of grapes used.

Some people might not like wine, or any alcoholic beverages for that matter. But believe it or not, there is a term for people who are afraid of wine. This fear is called oenophobia, the fear of wine. Enologists are wine chemists who analyze samples of wine and advise winemakers. Enology is the science of winemaking.

There was a time when wine was almost wiped out by nature. Phylloxera, a root parasite, was one of the biggest threats that the wine industry has faced. It put an axe to the roots of many vineyards around that time.

The phrase 'drinking to one's health' was rooted in the Greek custom in which the host of a dinner would take the first sip of wine to assure guests that the wine was not poisoned. Romans traditionally drop a piece of toasted bread into each glass of wine to prevent effects of too much acidity.

A mature wine's smell is called bouquet, while aroma is the term for the smell of a young wine. Women, having better smelling abilities, are better wine tasters, at least according to some research.

The color of the wine is determined through the grape skins. The absence or presence of skin during the fermentation dictates the product's color. Generally wine will be red when fermented with skin and white when fermented without the skin.

Drinking wine is a healthy habit, too. Studies have shown that the tendency to incur heart disease, Alzheimer's, and gum problems are reduced when people drink wine.

In 194 BC, a woman caught drinking wine was a good reason to get a divorce. In The Code of Hammurabi, a man guilty of faking wine or conducting any kind of wine fraud was punishable by being drowned in a river. Rome's decline has been blamed on chronic lead poisoning. Lead was used to improve the sweetness of a wine.

According to most research works, the top ten wine producing countries are Italy, France, Spain, United States, Argentina, Australia, South Africa, Germany, Chile, and Portugal.

In wine consumption, the states of California, New York, and Florida lead the United States of America.

In winemaking, swirling is done to release the powerful aroma in wines. The longer the after taste, the better the wine is. Grapes picked during a rainstorm make a wine taste diluted — watery.

Wine often brings out a different taste in food. Lighter wines are served first, then heavier wines next. White wine is served before red and younger wine before older. The year the wine is bottled is not necessarily its vintage year. A single year's harvest makes a vintage wine. A non-vintage wine is the product of two or more years of harvest. The heat of the hand raises the temperature of the wine in a glass. That's why the proper way to hold a wine glass is by its stem. Tutankhamen's tomb contained wine jars that were labeled in such a detailed manner that they may comply with the modern wine laws of several countries.

The Benefits Of Wine

As written above, wine has made a profound impact in the world's civilizations. It has marked its place in today's society.

It has been predicted that in the coming years, the consumption of wine will keep increasing. It was also projected that the production of specialty wines would make the market more exciting and more competitive.

Below you will find some benefits of drinking wine in moderation.

The risk of depression is reduced through moderate wine consumption. Men and women who consume at least two to eight glasses of wine each week tend to be less depressed.

Monks believed that drinking wine slows down aging. Resveratol, a compound that is found in the skin of blueberries, raspberries, and nuts, is an anti-aging compound that is also found in grape skins. Procyanidin is another compound found in red wines that keeps the blood vessels healthy. Red wines made in the traditional way contain a higher concentration of Procyanidin. It may help to prevent breast cancer and dementia; also improves cardiovascular health due to the presence of antioxidants in the seeds and skins of red grapes.

Severe sunburn may be prevented with the intake of wines and grapes. Flavonoids that are present in wines and grapes inhibits the formation of reactive oxygen species in skin cells that are exposed to sunlight.

When blood vessels in the eye grow uncontrollably, blindness can occur. Consumption of red wine may stop this phenomenon. It can help reduce the risk of heart attack and other heart diseases.

The Process of Winemaking

The technical term for winemaking is enology. It is Greek for a blend of the words study and wine.

Fermentation is a reaction in which yeast is combined to a liquid containing glucose (sugar), this in turn changes into carbon dioxide and ethanol. The alcohol content effecting this covers roughly 12-15% ethanol. Yeast can't live in stronger concentrations of ethanol.

Grapes rich in sugar content need to be used for successful fermentation to occur. There are up to 4,000 varieties of a grape species known as Vitis Vinifera, which is responsible for the majority of wines made worldwide.

Three Main Categories of Wine

1. Table Wines
2. Sparkling Wines
3. Fortified Wines

Red, white, or rose are examples of table wines. They are allowed to ferment naturally and comprise the bulk of the world's wine production. Sparkling and fortified wines are made by processes similar to the table wines, but extra steps are added to give the carbonation or extra alcohol desired.

A good harvest is just one part of the process. Winemaking is an extensive progression. Specific steps must be observed before the actual winemaking process can begin.

Winemaking's arch enemy: upsetting bacteria. Cleanliness and sanitation are indispensable in winemaking. The presence of troublesome bacteria can wreak havoc and result in unprecedented disaster.

Here is a brief overview of the process:

White Wine

White wine requires the grapes to be picked and immediately processed in the winepress. It takes about two hours to have the grapes gently squeezed and the juiced pumped into holding tanks. Once inside the tank, the juice is chilled and sediments settle to the bottom. When the sediments are removed, the wine is ready to be fermented with yeast. The juice is transferred to fermenting vats, and the yeast is added.

The juice is transferred to large vats where air is excluded. The growth of bacteria is discouraged and oxidation is prevented. Acetobecter has the ability to convert wine into vinegar overnight. Thus, it has its reputation as the most troublesome bacteria in winemaking.

Fermentation is a process that takes from a week to a month's period. Temperature must be maintained and observed. Different kinds of containers can be used for this process. One example is an oak barrel.

Sediments and dead yeast cells are separated. The wine is chilled to make the content clear. After this, it is transferred to bottles.

Red Wine

Grapes intended for red wine are initially processed in the crusher-destemmer. Must is the term used to describe the pulpy material that is left once the grapes have been separated from the stems and are gently crushed. The must is transferred into tanks or fermenting bins where it is left to cold soak for a few days. During cold soaking, the juice gains color and fruit flavor. Sulfur dioxide is then added to suppress the growth of wild yeast and other remaining bacteria.

During fermentation, carbon dioxide produced by fermentation pushes skins to the top of the tank or bin. The skins give the color and tannins varying degrees of astringency.

The method and the kind of grapes affects the time of the process. What comes after fermentation is to let sediments and dead yeast cells settle.

The wine is then separated from the skins. The wine is put into oak or redwood barrels for aging. Red wines are aged in different time spans. It could take from several months to several years.

Sparkling Wines

Sparkling wines, including champagne, are produced in the same way as white wines until fermentation is complete.

As the wines are put into bottles, more yeast and sugar are added. The airtight seal is placed on the bottles, preventing the carbon dioxide from escaping. Excess sediment on the wine must be removed through method champenoise.

Different Kinds of Wine

These are some of the common wines produced today.

PINOT GRIGIO (PEA-no GREE-gee-oh) Pinot Grigio is the Italian name for the French or American wine varietals known as Pinot Gris. Medium to full bodied, crisp, and dry with forward fruit.

RIESLING (REESE-ling) Riesling is a superb white wine grape from Germany that produces successfully in climates that are cooler. Produced at all levels of sweetness. Wonderfully crisp, light, dry wines.

MOSCATO (Muss-KAHT-oh) Moscato is fruity and very aromatic while at times displaying an effervescent or sparkling quality. It's taste is nearly always sweet and is thought to be one of the ancient grape varieties.

SAUVIGNON BLANC (So-veen-YOHN Blahnk) This is a white wine that is fresh and clean and typically has a fragrance as herbal or grassy.

CHARDONNAY (Shar-dun-NAY) This is a main stay in the wine world and varies from full bodied to light. Aromas and flavors tend to be fruity similar to orange, pineapple, apple or pear.

MERLOT (Mare-LOW) The homeland of Merlot is the Bordeaux region of France where it is the most planted vine variety. Produces a lush, plummy, velvety wine, typically medium bodied.

SANGIOVESE (San-Joe-VAY-zee) Sangiovese is Italy's most widely planted red grape and the heart of most central. Italian red wines, most notably Chianti and Brunello. Produces dense plumminess when grapes are fully ripe. Well-structured, often high-acid wines.

ZINFANDEL (ZIN-fan-dell) Red zinfandels range from fruity with light to medium body, to rich and powerful. Rich berry, black cherry, and plum aroma with a crisp, refreshing mouth feel.

SYRAH/SHIRAZ (Sir-AH/Shur-OZ) Shiraz is the Australian and South African name for the French variety known as Syrah. Produces ripe and often sweeter wines than Rhône-based wines, and a suggestion of chocolate as opposed to pepper and spices.

CABERNET SAUVIGNON (Cah-burr-NAY So-veen-YOHN) This is a popular and famous red wine, with the scent of black currants. It ages very well and yields subtle taste compounds.

PINOT NOIR (PEA-no Nwahr) Pinot Noir is the grape variety exclusively responsible for red Burgundy. The vine does better in cooler climates since the fruit ripens relatively early. Fruity at the core, essences like strawberry, cherry, and plum mingle with notes of sandalwood, spice, and flowers.

MALBEC (MAHL-beck) Malbec has become popular in Argentina, yet originated from France in the region of Bordeaux. It is a medium to full bodied wine, possesses earthy tannins and dark fruit flavors similar to plums.

Common Terminology

Here are some of the common terms in the world of wine:

You do not have to be lost in a conversation between enthusiasts. These are some of the most common terms you can hear between wine fanatics.

Acidity: This refers to a sour or tart flavor when the wine's acidity is high. Sometimes its described as tangy or tart.

Acrid: This can be a trait in red wines of poor quality, that possess overly acidic flavor.

Aftertaste: This is the taste that lingers and may be described as smooth, nonexistent, soft, lingering or harsh for example.

Aroma: This is referring to the scent of the specific grape variety in the wine.

Attractive: Usually describes a clean, fresh, light style of wine.

Balanced: Refers to correct proportions of wood, acid and fruit flavors, where none dominates the others.

Barnyard-y: A term for an earthy scent such as wet leaves or truffle. This particular quality is considered a negative.

Big: Describes a wine that might be dense, full bodied or the alcohol taste is more pronounced.

Bite: Refers to a definite tang of tannin or acidity. If it is experienced in the finish, it should possess a zestful quality and only in full-bodied, rich wines.

Bitter: This is considered a flaw if it dominates the aftertaste or flavor of the wine. It is one of the 4 basic tastes. A small amount experienced in sweet wines might enhance the balance. If it is found however in red young wines it may be a warning signal as this doesn't always disappear with the aging. An aged fine wine should not be bitter.

Body: This refers to the weight of the wine in your mouth, and is usually expressed as being light bodied, medium or full bodied.

Bouquet: This is the description of the aroma of the wine as it ages in the bottle.

Buttery: This trait is common in chardonnay wines, referring to both texture and flavor.

Character: Wines that possess top shelf traits.

Chewy: This term means full-bodied, heavy rich wines.

Crisp: A new wine with a fresh taste and good acidity levels.

Closed: Concentrated wines that contain character, but are lighter in flavor or scent.

Complete: Wines that are full bodied with a bold finish.

Complex: Refers to wines that are in harmony in regards to taste and flavor components.

Corked: This is when a wine smells like cork. It is not pleasing in either taste or smell. The wine will usually be dull and flat.

Delicate: Medium to light weight wines with quality taste.

Dense: A quality that is sought after in newer wines, concentrated scents on the palate and nose.

Depth: This is a term for a quality wine that is concentrated and complex with flavors that have subtle layers to them.

Developed: The age and maturity of wines.

Dirty: This is an indication of poor quality winemaking skills, and includes any odors that are bad in a wine, even those produced by corks or bad barrels.

Earthy: This trait is usually seen in red wines. It can be a positive or negative quality, depending on the context. Positive would be a pleasant description complementing the taste and smell of the wine.

On a negative note would be closer to dirty or barnyard-y.

Fading: This is a wine that is losing fruit, flavor or color usually due to aging.

Finish: This is similar to aftertaste, as it is the flavor that remains. An indicator of a good quality of wine is one that possesses a long finish.

Flabby: Not having enough acidity for taste and scent.

Flat: Similar to flabby, but is the stage beyond. Sometimes used to describe a bubbly wine that has lost its tickle.

Flinty: This refers to the smell of flint hitting steel in which some white wines may contain in smell or taste.

Fruity: Pretty self-explanatory here, sometimes it describes the taste of a specific fruit, and other times it suggests the wine is a little on the sweet side.

Full-Bodied: Has an almost thick or heavy sensation, it fills the mouth.

Graceful: This refers to a wine that is pleasing and everything is in good balance.

Green: The flavor of fruit unripe and not necessarily a fault.

Heady: The scent of a wine with a high alcohol level.

Herbaceous: A herbal smell or taste.

Legs: Is a description of the drops that slide down the sides of the glass when swirling a glass of wine. This is a sign of alcohol being there.

Length: This is also related to aftertaste, in that it refers to the amount of time that the flavor and scent linger after swallowing wine.

Mouth feel: This describe how the wine feels against the tongue, and in the mouth, it's texture.

Murky: Not clear and bright, a near cloudy type appearance.

Musty: An odor that is damp or moldy smelling.

Neutral: This is a wine that is really neither bad or good, just middle ground with nothing really standing out.

Oaky: The scent or flavor of oak.

Oxidized: Wines that are considered off or stale in some way.

Palate: This refers to the flavor and feel of the wine in the mouth.

Pedestrian: Simple, no frills.

Peppery: This refers to the flavor or white or black pepper in a wine. This trait is considered sharper than spicy.

Perfumed: Describes the overall delicate aroma of a wine.

Potent: This would be a wine that is intense and strong in some ways.

Quaffer: This is a wine intended to drink, not sip.

Robust: Wine that is both vigorous, strong and full bodied.

Round: This is a wine with a good balance of body, tannins and fruit.

Seductive: Wine that is very pleasing.

Short: This is a wine that doesn't last on the palate once it is swallowed.

Simple: A wine that tends to stay true to the first impression.

Smoky: A soft smoke from wood scent can sometimes be detected from either the aging process or barrel fermentation.

Soft: Refers to wine low in tannin, acid or alcohol and has minimal effect on the palate.

Spicy: In complex wines, sometimes there are spicy notes that can be detected such as mint, pepper, cloves, cinnamon or anise.

Supple: Another term for wine in good balance regarding fruit and tannin qualities.

Sweet: Sweet is one of the 4 basic flavors.

Tannin: This refers to a dry feel, often denoting tastes of tea or leather.

Tart: Very similar to acidity in description, a sharp taste.

Thin: Lacking depth and body, watery consistency.

Toasty: This trait is most commonly found in dry, white wines and refers to a slight flavor of wood from the barrel.

Velvety: Wines with this possess a very smooth texture and rich taste.

Zesty: A wine that is energizing.

Wine Tasting

You don't have to be an organoleptic to enjoy a glass of wine. All you need to have is the right knowledge on how to appreciate it better. Soon, it will come naturally for you.

The first thing is to hold the glass by its stem against a white background.

Pay attention to the shades of color.

By swirling, you maximize the wine's surface area and release more of the bouquet. Determine whether the wine is clean and attractive. Try to distinguish the intensity of the smell and what aroma comes to mind.

Vinegar smell is never a good sign. A cork smell means the wine has absorbed the taste of a defective cork. A sherry smell is the result of too much oxygen in wine. Sulfur indicates the formation of too much sulfur dioxide.

Take three seconds to hold the wine in your mouth before swallowing. Gauge whether the taste is more sweet, sour, bitter, alcoholic, or astringent overall. The way the wine feels in your mouth is called mouth feel and is a skill you could learn.

It is now the proper time to judge the wine. Look for the balance in the wine's totality and flavor. What do you think? What words come to mind as you ponder this?

How to Open a Bottle of Wine

Use a small knife to cut the seal off the bottle of wine, cleanly below the lip of the bottle, rotating as you go. Once that has been removed, hold the bottle at the neck, insert tip of a good corkscrew slightly off center and at a mild angle. This will help to minimize the cork from breaking.

Turn the corkscrew until it is fully inserted. Hook the corkscrew's lever on to the bottle's rim. Hold this lever in position with the thumb of the hand that holds the bottle. Lift the corkscrew up in a slow, firm, single motion until the cork is removed.

How Much to Buy

There is a simple formula to determine the right amount of wine you will need to ensure a successful party. First, determine the number of guests that will be coming to your event. Next, take the number of guests and multiply that by the number of hours the party is intended to last. This will give you the average number of servings you will need.

Example:

Number of Guests x Number of hours

= Number of Servings

5 guests x 2 hours = 10 Servings

To calculate how much wine to buy in relation to the number of servings for different bottle sizes, see the guide below:

3L bottle = 20 servings

1.5L bottle = 10 servings

750ml bottle = 5 servings

Example:

If you require 10 servings, you could

buy either one 1.5L bottle or two 750ml bottles.

The Benefits of Making Your Own Wine

Fine wine can be costly. You could spend a fortune on a few bottles. The good news is that the wine that is being consumed by more and more people is easy to make! Contrary to popular belief, making your own wine is not super complicated. You only need the ability to follow instructions well.

What keeps many people from tapping in to their resourceful side is fear, lack of knowledge, or perhaps lack of motivation. Well, fear no more; here are some of the benefits you will gain when you make your own wine.

With all the money you spend on those bottles of wine, the cost of the actual making of your own wine will blow your mind. Plus, you get to save bottles from your batches and open them on special occasions.

Since you can control the content in your wine, you can decide whether you want less sugar, or specific fruits. You can have the flavor you have always wanted. You can finally enjoy the taste you have been looking for.

Many folks find making wine a relaxing and enjoyable experience, so it can be stress-relieving.

Who can beat a gift of wine that you personally made? A bottle of wine is always a welcomed gift. Its a great feeling to give something you have personally made to a friend or loved one.

Besides having a hobby, you will enter a community of global winemakers. You will be a part of a group of enthusiastic people, possibly meeting others who share in the same passion.

Once you have finished a batch, you can't help but imagine ways to improve it until you reach perfection, so it is challenging in that regard. If a batch fails, it sets you on a learning expedition to uncover what went wrong.

It is an outlet for creativity, in finding new recipes to try, new combinations or techniques, and always a learning experience.

Common Misconceptions

It is a fact that whatever is popular or trendy tends to draw so much attention and attracts everybody's opinion on the subject. Winemaking is a trade that has existed for thousands of years. The increase in its consumption caught the attention of many entrepreneurs. Now the search for the next hit wine has many occupied.

Before we go to the instructions about winemaking, let us get ourselves familiar with some common misconceptions about wine and winemaking.

It has been widely believed that screw caps are cheap. Not anymore. Using screw caps eliminates the risk of your wine being contaminated by TCA, a compound that is dangerous to wines. Many winemakers today use this capping system as it reduces the risk of this happening. One of the misconceptions widely accepted these days is that corks are embraced to be the standard caps for wines. They are believed to contain special abilities that can age wine well. Australia's wine makers beg to differ. There is no logical reason why screw caps will not do well.

One common misconception is that sulfur in red wines gives you headaches. As long as allergies are not involved, chances are you are just plain dehydrated. Try making sure you are properly hydrated with water before drinking wine.

Next is the perception that expensive wines are better wines. Although this might often be the case, it is not necessarily always true.

Another misconception is that mass produced wines are good but never great. There is no need to elaborate on this. Huge budget and top notch facilities are two things that might give a company an edge in winemaking. Obviously, corporations have these.

Boutique wines have gained a lot of popularity these days. They made authenticity their foundation. While certain unique processes and factors come into play, does this guarantee a better product?

Another common misconception is that there is a right time to open a bottle. While there are some wines that do require a specific time to be opened, most wines can be enjoyed the moment they are released.

The thicker the legs, the better the wine. When you swirl a glass of wine, the 'tears' that flow down the glass are also considered the wine's legs. This however is not a reliable gauge for good quality. What is actually happening when this is seen is the alcohol evaporating faster and possessing a lower surface tension than water. The legs are driven up the glass due to the increased surface tension before its is pulled back down by gravity force. Generally full-bodied wines will experience slower dripping rates of the legs than other wines.

Wine making at home is difficult and takes a lot of time. Making your own wine has never been easier. Known winemakers have included wine kits in their products that have encouraged a lot of enthusiasts to explore the world of wine making. It only takes about a month to finish a batch of wine.

Expensive equipment is necessary. With the advanced technology we have today thanks to passionate inventors, the processes in winemaking, like crushing fruits, has never been easier. Well, actually, you don't have to crush fruits as juices for winemaking have already been made for you.

Here is the biggest one so far: making your own wine is illegal.

Is it legal to make my own wine? Winemaking, also known as home brewing, is legal in the U.S. and many other places provided:

1. You annually produce only 100 gallons of wine (or less) by yourself; up to 200 gallons if you live in a household with another adult.

2. You do not sell your homemade wine.

3. You must be 21 or legal drinking age to make and drink your homebrew.

4. You may not distill hard alcohol.

5. You can taste and share homebrewed beer and wines.

Practical Things To Remember

If you are affected by conditions such as liver failure or heart failure, refrain from drinking wine. Check your allergies, especially with sulfites. Drinking and driving have never been friends, do not do so under any circumstance. Do not drink while pregnant. Consult your doctor if you are unsure how alcohol will interact with any drugs you are taking.

What Kind of Grapes Do I Use?

Wines are not made from the seedless table grapes we find in our local grocery stores. Grapes that are specific to wine making are used. There are over 4,000 different wine grape varieties that are used in making wine. Each type brings a different trait to the finished wine. It is beyond the intended scope of this e-book to cover all of these, and likely would take years of study on this topic alone. Therefore, we will list a few of the most common, popularly used wine grape varieties.

Red Wine Grapes

Cabernet Sauvignon - This grape produces a wine that is medium to full-bodied and high in tannins. Many times it is mixed with other wine grapes to mellow it a bit.

Zinfandel - Many people may assume this type of grape is white, due to the popularity of White Zinfandel wines, but it really is a red grape. It makes dark, rich wines that are high to medium in tannin and high in alcohol content. Some are successful in young wines, and others need a good maturing process.

Shiraz or Syrah - These grapes create deep colored wines, full-bodied and a firm tannin with complex flavors.

Pinot Noir - This can be difficult to grow, but worth the effort. These grapes make a wine that is lighter in color than Merlot and Cabernet. It possesses high to medium acidity, low to medium tannin, and fairly high alcohol.

Merlot - These grapes produce a wine that is full-bodied, low tannin, high alcohol and deep in color.

White Wine Grape Varieties

Pinot Gris/Pinot Grigio - The skin of this grape type is darker than usual for a white wine variety. The wine from these grapes are usually full to medium bodied, neutral scent and fairly low acidity.

Sauvignon Blanc - These grapes produce a wine fairly high in acidity, with strong flavors and scents.

Riesling - The grapes can produce white wines that are either sweet or dry. They usually have medium to low alcohol levels, light-bodied, high acidity and refreshing.

Chardonnay - This white grape carries different fruity tones depending on the climate it is grown in, and some also possess earthy scents. The wine will have high to medium acidity and full-bodied usually. They typically are dry wines.

What Kind of Equipment Do I Need?

There are many options out there for winemaking equipment, from elaborate systems to very primitive components. It can be quite confusing when starting out to find which would work best. We will list the equipment you'll need to make your own wine. On a few items, we will list a couple of options for you to choose from. You may want to visit a wine making store, or order some of them online. However, you decide to gather your equipment, be sure that you have everything you need before you even attempt the actual wine making process. For some, buying a simple winemaking kit might be the route to go.

Since this guide is for beginners, we are going to keep things simple in regards to equipment. There are more advanced equipment and tool options out there, you might want to try down the line.

Essentially, there will be 2 fermentation processes, so you'll need a container for each.

1. You will need a 2 gallon glass jar or crock for the first fermentation, just make sure they are not scratched on the inside. It could also be a plastic bucket, provided the bottom says 1 or 2 for recycling, that is critical. If you use a plastic bucket like the one listed here, be sure to get an airlock and rubber stopper also (see below) that will fit the drilled hole, to allow fermenting gas to escape.

2. A glass 1 gallon carboy, this is a large glass jar with a neck. For only a couple dollars more, you could get a 1 gallon carboy with an airlock, which you will need. The choice basically is to buy it together or separately.

3. Empty wine bottles and either corks or screw lids to fit these, for your finished wine.

4. Airlock (they have these as well as the other wine making equipment needs at Amazon.com) - This is a device that is put on top of the glass jar carboy fermentation process (2nd one), that allows the fermentation gas to escape, but allows no air to come into the jar. Airlocks are very inexpensive. You just need to make sure that you have a good sealing rubber stopper or lid for your glass carboy that will hold your airlock. Sometimes having an extra on hand is worthwhile too, especially if you need to later sweeten your wine more that originally was done.

5. Auto-siphon - another very inexpensive tool, used to transfer your wine during various stages.

6. Long handle plastic spoon for stirring.

7. Campden tablets - This is sodium/potassium metabisulfite (sodium metabisulfite is not recommended, be sure to get the potassium type), and are very inexpensive. It is imperative to use them when working with fresh fruit or when you plan to use sorbates. Potassium metabisulfite is what the vast majority of wineries use. Campden tablets kill bacteria, mold, and limits growth of wild yeast. assisting the correct wine yeast to freely grow and helps protect your wine. They also are a method to sanitize your wine making equipment.

8. Clean cheesecloth and a large rubber band, big enough to fit around your 2 gallon crock.

9. Funnel

10. Turkey baster

11. Wine yeast - this is not the same as bread yeast! Do not use bread yeast, it will not make a good wine.

12. Mortar & pestle and plastic measuring spoons.

13. Potato masher

14. Small glass bowl to dissolve Campden tablet in.

15. Lots of soap and hot water, and sanitizer.

We will go into sanitizers in the next chapter as it is a critical component to successful wine making. We will list the food ingredients needed as we get closer to making the wine.

What About Sanitization?

Sanitization is vitally important in wine making, it is a very attractive environment for bacteria, molds and wild yeast to grow. If these get into your wine at any point, the wine will turn into vinegar or otherwise be ruined. This is probably THE most important aspect to successful winemaking there is. If you are going to go through the process to make wine, you want to ensure that you do it correctly, and this is the correct foundation; properly sanitized conditions.

While there are many methods and options available to clean and sanitize equipment, I'm going to keep it simple and use my favorite methods, but will offer several options.

Cleaning and sanitization are not the same thing. You are looking at a two step process. Cleaning is the removal of dirt, grime and residue that is usually visible to the eye and needs to be removed before sanitizing. It is the first step in the process.

Sanitizing is the process of treating your equipment chemically, that not only eradicates but helps prevent the growth of wild yeasts, bacteria and molds.

At every point in your wine making endeavor, be sure to wash and scrub your hands thoroughly with hot water and soap. Before starting you wine making, you need to clean and sanitize every part of every single item that will come into contact with your wine process, including turkey baster, airlocks, auto-siphons, carboys, tubes, stirrers, cheesecloth, funnels, bottles, corks or lids, rubber band, everything. A good wipe down of the surface areas you will be working on is also important.

For the first cleaning step, I like to use a chemical cleaner with a soak, then gently scrub the parts I can. The reason I prefer this is some parts in an airlock or other pieces can be difficult to reach for a good scrub, and yet this gets them clean.

Both products recommended are called percarbonates, which are a blend of hydrogen peroxide and sodium carbonate and other ingredients. They work with a mild alkali and active oxygen to lift dirt and grime. They are also easy on the septic system and environmentally friendly. P.B.W. use 2 oz. in 5 gallons of warm water, soak your equipment for 30 minutes, then rinse. Straight A cleanser use at 1 Tablespoon per gallon of water, soak for 30 minutes, then rinse. This is also good for removing labels off glass.

Next you will need to sanitize all your equipment. This can be done immediately after cleaning if desired. Although chlorine may be used, very thorough rinsing is critical and if it's not properly rinsed everywhere, it could ruin your wine. The sanitizers listed below are all very reasonably priced and worth not having to be so critical on rinsing.

The Campden tablets listed above, are potassium metabisulfite and is an excellent sanitizer of your wine equipment, again this means all items. If you buy the tablet form, simple crush with a mortar & pestle into a fine powder, or you can purchase the powdered form. Mix 8 teaspoons per 1 gallon a water, allow your equipment to soak for 5 minutes, then allow to drip dry. No rinsing needed.

A second method for sanitizing is with an iodine product called Iodophor. Its used in both the medical industry and food service to sanitize equipment. Make a solution of 1 Tablespoon per gallons of water, then soak all equipment for 10 minutes, then drip dry. No rinsing necessary. This will stain fabric however, so you will need to be careful about that.

Another popular option is a product called Star-San, this foams readily getting into cracks and crevices, odorless, flavorless and biodegradable. Will not affect your wine negatively in any way. Mix 1 ounce per 5 gallons of water, soak your equipment for 1 minutes, then drip dry. No rinsing needed.

Now that all your equipment is gathered, cleaned and sanitized, you are ready to begin. You will want to ensure that you have all your food ingredients on hand as well, coming up next.

Time to Make the Wine

Food Ingredients:

16 cups of fruit - this can be wine grapes, any other type of fruit, or a combination of several fruits

2 cups sugar or honey

1 packet of wine yeast

1 Campden tablet

Couple of gallons of distilled water

1. Prepare the fruit. If possible use organic fruit so you are not dealing with pesticides. Wash the fruit, remove stems and leaves, and place in the crock, or your plastic bucket for 1st fermentation. Do not peel the skins as they carry alot of flavor. Now mash the fruit with either your clean hands, or a potato masher, keep crushing to release the juice from the fruit. Try to get it about 2-3 inches from the top of the crock. If you are a bit short, you can top it off with some distilled water until it reaches that point in the crock.

2. Take 1 Campden tablet and crush it into a very fine powder in your mortar and pestle. Then add this fine powder to 1/2 cup of distilled water and stir thoroughly until it is dissolved. Once it is dissolved, pour this into your crushed fruit crock and stir well.

3. Add the honey or sugar. If you are using sugar (you can use white or brown), add it first to 1 cup boiling distilled water and stir to thoroughly dissolve. Then pour into the fruit mixture and stir. You can add more sugar later in the process if you find you want the wine sweeter, or if you know you

like a sweeter wine, you could start with 3 cups of sugar or honey. The sweetener helps to feed the yeast.

4. Add the wine yeast. Open 1 packet of the wine yeast and add it to your fruit mixture. Use your long handled plastic stirrer and stir well. This mixture is now called a 'must.'

5. Ferment the Wine

    If you are using a plastic bucket, now is the time to put the lid on, the rubber stopper and airlock. If you are using a crock, cover it with cheesecloth and secure it with a large rubber band that will fit around the crock. Let it sit overnight in an area between 70 - 75 degrees. Try not to let it get cooler that 70 degrees.

6. The next day, uncover and stir gently yet thoroughly, then re-cover your crock or bucket. Repeat this every 4 hours the first day. The following 3 days do the same thing a few times per day. The 'must' will bubble as yeast moves into action. This is the fermentation process. Be sure to thoroughly wash your hands and sanitize your plastic stirrer each time.

7. After the 4 days and the bubbling slows, it's time to siphon and strain the must. Get your sanitized carboy glass jar out and your auto-siphon. To strain the solids out, you can place a sterile funnel into the carboy and line it with some cheesecloth. As you siphon the must out of the crock, let it run over the cheesecloth, into the funnel and into the glass jar. Whenever you transfer the must from one container to another, that is called racking, or 'rack your wine.'

8. Remove the funnel and now insert your air-lock onto the carboy. You will need to fill the inside of the air-lock

(according to manufacturer's directions) with a sterile liquid such as vodka or sterile distilled water. The air-lock allows the release of fermentation gas, while keeping oxygen out.

9. Second fermentation begins. Place your carboy in a safe, out of the way place and allow it to sit undisturbed for about 1 month in temps between 65 - 75 degrees. Occasionally, check your air-locks to ensure they are still firmly in place and that the sanitized liquid is still there. If it's getting low, add more to the air-lock.

If you find that foam has risen up into the air-lock, don't fret. Remove it, clean and sanitize it then put it back on. It's nice to have an extra sanitized air-lock on hand for this purpose, that you can quickly and simply replace the one with foam in it. Do this as quickly as you can to minimize exposure to oxygen.

When the wine has become clear, at about 4 - 5 weeks of aging, it is ready for taste testing. If it is still cloudy, give it a couple more weeks.

10. Taste testing and adjusting. Take your sanitized turkey baster and draw out some wine into a glass. Keep the air-lock clean and nearby. Taste your wine. If you like it, go on to step 11.

If the wine needs to be sweeter, draw out 2 cups of wine with the turkey baster.

Make a simple syrup by boiling 4 cups of distilled water and 4 pounds of sugar. Stir until dissolved, then allow to cool.

Into your 2 cup wine sample, add 1/2 oz. of the simple syrup and mix. Taste. Keep doing this until it reaches your desired sweetness, keeping track of how many 1/2 oz increments you used. Once the wine tastes where you want it to be, add 4 fl. oz. of the simple solution per gallon of wine made, to your carboy jar per 1/2 oz. you used to sweeten your sample. Stir your wine with a sanitized stirrer.

Drink or discard your sample, do not return it to the carboy jar.

11. Add another Campden tablet; crush it into a very fine powder in your mortar and pestle. Then add this fine powder to 1/4 cup of distilled water and stir thoroughly until it is dissolved. Pour this into your carboy jar, stir thoroughly with a sanitized stirrer, then re-seal with your air-lock.

12. Wait about a week or so, then when the wine is clear again, use your auto-siphon and fill into your sanitized glass wine bottles. Try to keep the siphon off the very bottom of the carboy and leave the sediment there (either toss that last bit of sediment out when you clean up, or strain the last bit with a coffee filter). Cork or cap the bottles and label. Red wines should be stored in darker wine bottles to help preserve the color.

You can now enjoy your wine anytime you want, or continue to age it for months to years in the bottle. It should be stored in fairly constant, cooler temperatures about 55 degrees ideally, preferably in a darkened setting on the bottle's side.

Common Mistakes

Human error. We just can't avoid it. Often it is already too late before we realize we have made a mistake. Then we have no choice but either to quit or do it all over again.

The Wrong Equipment. Winemaking requires certain conditions to be met. Therefore, you need the right equipment to meet those conditions to achieve the best possible results. Centuries of winemaking have led us to homebrew stores that house equipment for both starters and the experienced wine makers.

Undetermined sample size. So, you have already bought the things you will need, jumped right to the process, and started mixing stuff and all. Then you realize that the yeast is not enough and certain chemicals do not look well.

It is best to plan ahead and plan strategically. Apart from saving money on the things that you do not need a great amount of, determining the exact amount of what you need prevents second thinking during the actual process. Focused means less mistakes.

Poor Sanitation. If there is one thing that will ruin your wine within hours, it is poor sanitation. Dirt and unwanted bacteria is your enemy. Your wine could turn into vinegar in no time. Do everything and treat your equipment with sanitation in mind. Maintain cleanliness and you will be fine.

Yeast-less production. Without yeast, it is impossible for you to make a successful wine.

Refill sanitized liquid when it is gone from the airlock. Remove, clean, and sanitize the airlocks. Keep a spare airlock, just in case.

Once the mixture becomes clear, it is ready for tasting and drinking.

Conclusion

Winemaking has an extensive role in our history. Perhaps the fruit-picking nomads began it all. We can never be sure as to how it all began. One thing we can be sure about is the fact that the industry of winemaking has proven to be one that is in demand and still growing.

The craft itself has been through different hurdles that have almost banished it to extinction. Nevertheless, it survived. The love for wine and the passion for its taste have pushed the industry to its limits. Nevertheless, the results were astonishing and productive.

There is no reason to back away from making your own wine. It could be one of the most enjoyable things you've done in a long time. Ready to begin?

If you enjoyed this book or received value from it in any way, would you be kind enough to leave a review for this book on Amazon? I would be so grateful. Thank you!

Printed in Great Britain
by Amazon